CH00666372

NOW THAT YOU ARE FORMLESS

Contemplations For Self-Revelations

HELEN HAMILTON

BALBOA.PRESS
A DIVISION OF HAY HOUSE

Balboa Press books may be ordered through booksellers or by contacting:

Balboa Press
A Division of Hay House
1663 Liberty Drive
Bloomington, IN 47403
www.balboapress.co.uk
UK TFN: 0800 0148647 (Toll Free inside the UK)
UK Local: 02036 956325 (+44 20 3695 6325 from outside the UK)

Because of the dynamic nature of the Internet, any web addresses or
links contained in this book may have changed since publication and may
no longer be valid. The views expressed in this work are solely those
of the author and do not necessarily reflect the views of the publisher,
and the publisher hereby disclaims any responsibility for them.

The author of this book does not dispense medical advice or
prescribe the use of any technique as a form of treatment for physical,
emotional, or medical problems without the advice of a physician,
either directly or indirectly. The intent of the author is only to offer
information of a general nature to help you in your quest for emotional
and spiritual well-being. In the event you use any of the information
in this book for yourself, which is your constitutional right, the author
and the publisher assume no responsibility for your actions.

Any people depicted in stock imagery provided by Getty Images are
models, and such images are being used for illustrative purposes only.
Certain stock imagery © Getty Images.

Print information available on the last page.

ISBN: 978-1-9822-8319-3 (sc)
ISBN: 978-1-9822-8320-9 (e)

Balboa Press rev. date: 02/22/2021

CONTENTS

DEDICATION

This book is offered in the hopes that it will help to end suffering. By bringing the revelation of our true nature into an experiential reality, we can spread light across all humanity.

CHAPTER 1

Introduction

This book will be most useful for those who have done a certain amount of self-inquiry and have come to realise that they cannot find themselves anywhere when they look. It will also be useful for those who have accidentally stumbled upon the fact that the person they have taken themselves to be is not real, nor was it ever. However, this book will be useful to anyone on a spiritual pathway that is dedicated to full enlightenment, or Self-Realisation, no matter where they think they have progressed to.

The purpose of this book is to help bridge a gap that seemed to appear for the author upon realisation of the formlessness. There had been many recognitions of the true nature of myself as being emptiness, formlessness or nothingness. It had been seen many times by myself that the person I thought I was, simply did not exist. The person was a thought-construct and so was all its expectations, beliefs, resistances, hopes and dreams.

After seeing this, there was a huge impact upon the experience of living and fear began to vanish along with doubts, desires and much more. After an initial "honeymoon" period this change seemed to slow right down and there was some restlessness in the being again as if some answer was still missing. Over time, I began to question why that was and why I was not living as the sages of old did. It seemed that some ingredient was missing. I began to become very curious about this and what was happening. An urgency to find out developed and it suddenly became urgent that I find out what it meant to be formless.

Now, "what it means to be formless" cannot simply be what you think about it because that is happening in thought and form only. It occurred to me that I must become at least as interested in what it is like to fully realise formlessness as I was previously interested in believing I was a person. I had to become devoted to my own formlessness with the vigour, conviction and passion with which I had once believed I was a separate entity alone in time and space. I began to realise that at some point, I must have spent a considerable amount of time ignoring my formlessness as an infant and focused only on the body, form and what it felt like to be a "someone" moving around in time and space. I began to wonder if this is what the sages had done and I recalled the Buddha sitting under the Bodhi tree with delight. I suddenly knew what Christ had gone into the desert for. It was suddenly obvious that I must develop a single-minded focus on living AS formlessness itself and all that this involved. In short, I must reverse the process I had unknowingly undertaken as an infant in this body. I began to notice such descriptions from all the awakened beings of all ages that I had read about or encountered. I would read such things as "Just stay as the witness" or "stay as the Self" or even "be nothing". Sri Ramana Maharshi's highest teaching was his silence but if we could not recognise that he would simply tell us to "be still".

Questions

I noticed that when something happened in the world outside or some inner response was triggered that a question arose inside me spontaneously. I asked myself, "how would this affect me if I was formless?" Each time the same answer came. The more interested I became in this, the more questions began to come. Such as "what do I have to do about this?" and "is this relevant to me still from here? I began to contemplate everything that happened to the mind and body and held it up to be examined in the light of these questions; after all, if I was truly the infinite formless presence then I could not keep thinking I still had things to transcend, to let go of, or to work through. I could not even keep believing that I had to deepen my experience of living as this.

I realised I was being asked to make a choice every moment of whether to live as a form or as myself, the formless One.

I have written this book to help bring light to this stage and to present the questions that really systematically helped me. There seemed to be very little written by the sages to explain this stage of realisation. Only simple remarks such as "stay as the witness" as described before. It is my aim with this book to speed the process of falling totally in love with yourself as you really are and to let go of all delusion.

The rest of the book presents one idea per chapter. Contemplate whichever one feels most magnetic to you right now, and in the end, you will see that all the chapters are the same. Each idea is designed to help you live as you really are – to fully live as the infinite nature you are. It is one thing to know you are infinite, timeless, deathless, sentience itself; and another to realise the implications of this and the joy it can bring. Work through them all, if you can, as contemplating each chapter will be simultaneously working on all the others! Over time, the process itself will become so joyful and exciting to you that you will not want to stop.

Contemplation is simply asking a thought question and experiencing the answer. The first thing that will happen is that you receive a thought answer to your question. Then you may receive an emotional answer and finally an experiential answer. When you receive an experiential answer you must stay very interested in this. Ask again and again until you are so used to the experiential answer, that it feels obvious. It may even begin to feel absurd or strange to ask the question anymore but stay with it.

The final realisation of this will be that each question can become a lifetime of joyful study and that no answer you receive is final. The joy of the manifest expression of you is that for each question you can experience an ever-deepening answer that can never come to an end. You can choose to spend the rest of your life on an inner investigation as to what it is like to live as yourself. This becomes more and more delightful as you continue. Try it and see!

CHAPTER 2

Confirmation of Your Formlessness

If you have already confirmed that you are formless through some inner revelation or self-inquiry then this chapter can be lightly read and you may want to move on to the rest of the book. If, however, you still do not know this or still have a tendency to think of yourself as a person, or a someone, then this chapter needs to be fully read, digested and assimilated before continuing. Each chapter builds upon this one and this is the foundation.

If you simply read this chapter and keep interested in seeing ever more about yourself, then you may not even feel a pull to read any further. In the final seeing, it will be revealed to you from inside that all the chapters are explaining the same thing and are coaxing you to become very curious about what you really are. As humans, we are curious by our very nature, but this curiosity can often be diverted by the mind at a time just before real seeing is about to occur. Staying interested in this book or finding a true teacher that has already realised this and can guide you is vital at this point. Simply the wish to wake up fully will bring a teacher to you. Be sure their words resonate in your heart as true.

How to Know That You Are Formless

When we look at ourselves and try to actually see what we are, we will not find a person or a solid object. Of course we find a body is present in our awareness. Thoughts may also be present, as well as emotions and other sensations in the body. There is a feeling of "I" that is aware of the body, thoughts and sensations, but what is this "I" actually? All our lives, we have been encouraged to believe that we are this body and mind, but this simply cannot be true because you are aware of them. Whatever you can perceive or observe, you cannot be.

If we scan inside our being to find this "I" that is trying to wake up or is struggling with some emotion or problem, we might be surprised! Scanning ourselves is not the same as thinking about ourselves. It is a direct looking to see, not thinking or analysing, what we are. Looking for this "I" does not involve thinking at all.

Take a moment right now to see if you can actually find yourself and you may be surprised to notice that you cannot actually find yourself! Obviously, you are here, because something is operating this body and is able to search for itself, but you are not what you thought yourself to be. As we continue to look again and again, we may come to realise that what "I" am is not an object. "I" is not a thing that we can find. In fact, we begin to see that what we are is no-thing. We are the subjective watcher, or witness. We are formless and forms are appearing inside us.

Fear Response

It's quite common to feel fear at this revelation but we should not let this halt our investigation into what we are. There might be fear, but this is simply because we are so used to thinking that we know what we are. If we ask anybody what or who they are, then we will probably get some very strange looks and answers, such as "I am me, obviously" or "I am a human being". For the first time in our lives we find ourselves unsure of what we are and this can make us feel scared. If we allow this revelation to deepen and come into the heart of our being, it can immediately begin to bring peace; for if we are formless, then we cannot suffer, age or even die! It can be strange to see our own self is already immortal and our mind can reject this.

You would not be reading a book such as this if you were destined to let this fear response stop you. You must go all the way and come home completely and once you have made this discovery that you are not a person, you can read on and begin to realise the sweet fruits of your inner looking.

Remember, you are simply now realising how you have always been and nothing has really changed!

CHAPTER 3

Consciously Be Yourself

Everybody is already the pure awareness Self of all that is. There never was any separation or merging with God. You have never been born or died in any lifetime. You only have had this One life that has been Always-ness, beyond time. All bodies come and go in you, noticed by you. Everything passes but you. All forms seem to appear, to change and to disappear; from the most subtle energetic forms to thoughts, emotions, physical bodies and inanimate objects. All this is you and you are in all this.

So why do most people spend their entire lives unaware of this and suffering? Because they don't know that they are living in illusion. They believe their minds and actually think that being a separate human being, travelling through time and space, to the end of their lives and then dying is the only option. You are finding out differently now and you must make a choice to live in this new way.

Even at this stage, many people have a glimpse of awakening or an experience of what it is like to live as yourSelf, yet few actually come to live consciously as the true Self that we are. This true Self is a stateless state of pure awareness, pure sentience before form and is aware of the universes coming and going. In this "place", there is no idea of separation or union. No duality. No time or space or movement. There is no difference here, and there is nothing other than this Self – you. There is only you and knowing this and living as this brings utter contentment and peace.

During my awakening, a great deal of time seemed to be wasted trying to find out what I had to "do" to wake up so fully that the idea of falling asleep again could not even enter my consciousness. I wanted to know what the Sages and Avatars had done that I had not as yet. What was this crucial difference that took one beyond the ideas of separation and coming home again permanently? What was it they must have undertaken in order to live in the place where none of this ever was true? I realised that the way to make the total and final cross over to the Self and only the Self was to **consciously spend time as the Self.**

The Abode of the Sages

When we consistently spend time each day simply being the field of awareness, the power of that true place begins to erase all delusion from our consciousness. We can either spend the rest of our lives transcending a never-ending stream of problems that our mind presents to us or we can allow the power of the true Self to do it for us. It involves spending as much time as you can each day simply being aware of yourself consciously as being formless and timeless. We all spend all our lives *unconsciously* being our True Self but when we are conscious of what is really here and put attention on it, then we begin to experience powerful change in the changeless that we are.

The Sages realised that the only remedy for our illusion was to live in and AS the true Self and to let this powerful love remove any traces of anything other than the Truth. To confirm that we are formless and not, in fact, separate from anything is merely the first step. And in fact, it means nothing if we are simply going to spend each day living from the mind and delusion. Even if we spend our lives praying and beseeching God to take away illusion, He cannot do it for us without our help. Our part is to be the Truth consciously long enough, consistently, until nothing else remains.

Until nothing "else" remains.

Until nothing other than Truth remains.

There is nothing other than Truth. To try to eradicate falsehood or illusion only perpetuates it.

To try to *become* the true Self will only cause more illusion, because you already are it.

To have a deep desire to merge with God is necessary at first, but now it will only keep you seemingly separate. The merging is simply living as if you were never separate.

To plead with God, awakened Beings or teachers to remove illusion from you is to only verify its reality even more. The thing about illusion is that it is not real! Anything you do to try to remove illusion only makes it *appear* more real and what is real will appear further away.

Only one decision remains then. Will you stay consciously as yourSelf long enough to be totally free? Will you stay as the field of infinite potential and treat every delusion that comes up to be looked at with the same simple medicine of being yourSelf? Will you accept that you cannot fix the "I" that does not actually exist? Will you make the effort to stay this simple as much as is needed? This is what Christ did in the desert. This is what Buddha did under the Bodhi tree.

Every second you spend looking at what you really are and being it is undoing lifetimes of delusion effortlessly. Things will fall away from you without you ever lifting a finger. Continue living your life and do what needs to be done, but inside you must stay as the awareness only. Be the nothingness. Choose to live as if you were already totally empty and see what happens.

To aid this commitment and to support you in your endeavour, know that all kinds of help will come and this book is one of them. The rest of this book will encourage you to consciously be yourSelf by showing you the aspects of being formless and undivided that perhaps have not as yet fully pervaded your consciousness. All the power of the Universe is with you.

PRESENCE PAUSE

Awareness is always here

While maintaining a relaxed but alert watchfulness, let the thought "awareness comes and goes" arise and watch it carefully without losing yourself in it.

• Is the thought inside the aware intelligence that is the knower of the thought, or is the thought outside of that?

• Is there any difference between the thought itself and the aware intelligence that knows it?

• Stay with the thought and especially watch when the thought ends. Does the awareness witnessing both the movement of the thought and the stillness of no thought, change in any way?

Allow, be curious, be open, and notice the space in which all thoughts, emotions and manifestations rise and fall. Rest in this simple wakefulness again and again until you are satisfied that awareness is always here in spite of what appears and disappears in and on it.

CHAPTER 4

You Are Effortlessly Here

Take a moment before you begin reading to tune in to your real Self.

Dropping any thoughts, expectations, history, problems, anticipations and desires for a moment will allow you to see what you cannot drop. That is your real Self. A simple, vast and powerful space of awareness that is simply here.

If you look for your separate sense of self in this space you will not find it. Whenever you look for yourself you will find only This That Is. This IS your real Self. It is invisible, intangible and formless. Look and confirm for yourself again that this is you.

Notice that you are effortlessly here. You are simply here and you are not exerting any effort to be here. You are not doing any technique or practice to be here. If you simply stay as this, then it is always effortless.

What does it mean to be effortless? Have you really considered that? It means that you are here without any other support. It means that you are not needing anything else to allow you to live. Being the effortless one means that you exist independently of everything. It means that if the whole manifest universe disappeared right now you would still be here and unaffected. Allow this to be digested and question these statements until what is said in these chapters is obviously true in your experience.

Being the effortless One means that you cannot run out of energy, that you have never been exhausted, you cannot get tired or sleepy. It also means that you will never need anything at all to be here always. A car needs petrol eventually or it stops and a human body needs food eventually but you need absolutely nothing.

Keep looking at what it means to be effortless here and confirm that whatever is making effort is the mind and not you. This silent space of awareness is simply here now and watching without any specific interest. Even when great effort is made by the body or mind, it is watched in this effortless place that you are.

This means that you are safe. Nothing and nobody can cause you to stop existing if you don't need anything to help you exist. You cannot run out of battery or exhaust yourself if you are effortless already and always have been.

This means that your survival has never been in question and will always be effortlessly continuous. You are even beyond "sustaining" yourself as you are without beginning.

Once you examine the truth of these statements and come to live them experientially, then you will live in joy and clarity. Effortlessly, you exist always and once you become aware of that which needs no sustaining, you will be happy.

Scientists have searched for years to find a clean, free and sustainable source of energy, all the while not knowing that they are the source of all energy and it is inexhaustible and unable to be used up; never-ending and present in an infinite supply. We can see the evidence of this unlimited power when we managed to build an atomic bomb and set it off; or when we have managed to split an atom. This has always been here.

CHAPTER 5

Embracing Your Formlessness

As we start this contemplation of our Self, let us look again for what we are. Searching for what we actually are or asking the question "what am I?" should take us to an immediate noticing that we are not a thing.

Not being a thing will allow us to release all fear once we have fully looked at and digested this knowledge deep inside. Only things have beginnings and endings. Only forms have a birth and a death. We can immediately see that we find no entity when we look at ourselves. There is simply an invisible, intangible but very definitely present awareness that is what we are. Awareness has no form although many forms appear in it.

The more we look and confirm that we are formless in our essential nature, the clearer it will be that we are not subject to birth, life and death. In fact, we will come to see that birth, life and death are all happening to our body only and we are the Immortal witness of this.

This may seem very grandiose but it becomes obvious and simple the more you contemplate it. The body appeared from somewhere and is sustained by something other than

17

it. Something must have been here before the body and it is that same invisible and formless you that is making the lungs breathe and the heart beat.

Realising this will bring a profound change in your life because you will no longer fear an end to you. Beginnings and endings happen inside you but not to you. You did not start and therefore you cannot end. Immortality is already your nature and you have always been safe. Nothing can harm you or hurt you when you have no form.

Continue in your investigations into what it really means to be formless until you have fully realised that this is the key to freedom. Never assume that you have seen all there is to see. You can always have a deeper understanding about yourself; you are the source of all understanding.

You may find such questions as "How can I really know I cannot die?" or "How do I know I was not born?" helpful. Feel around inside yourself and find a question that really resonates with you. Questions can be extremely helpful to find areas where you doubt your realisation still and can achieve greater clarity.

It's totally ok to feel as though you can't as yet totally confirm that you cannot die; it is simply a call to investigate further until you are convinced. You will know when you are making progress as there will be an absence of fear and an expanding sense of freedom and joy.

CHAPTER 6

Discovering You Have No Location

As you check in with yourself and find the "you" that has no form or shape, you might begin to notice that you cannot find yourself in any particular location. You are obviously here to search for yourself but when you look, what you find is the you that has no location.

What does this mean for you? It means you cannot say that you are only here in this body; that can no longer be true for you. It also means you cannot say that you are beyond the body as that involves a location of "everywhere but the body". These statements may seem weird, wrong or true but either way you must not stop your contemplation until you have experienced their truth.

If you keep looking and finding no location you will also come to know that the categories of thought such as "everywhere" and "nowhere" also do not apply to you. Which of these are you? Neither? Both? Beyond both? All these thoughts have been used to describe you, but they really do not apply to this location-less you.

Have another look as you read and notice that you are not even simply "here" unless you really broaden what you mean by here. "Here" also brings in the possibility of "not here" too and this is not the case for you. Aren't you always here when you look for you? Don't you always seem to notice that you are here even before you look for what you are?

Contemplating these points deeply will bring you to an experiential knowingness that is irrefutable. It will show you that you are inside everything and everything is also inside you. Which is most true? Both and neither.

As you come to see that you are all-pervading and that you are not absent anywhere in the universe you will begin to see there is nothing "other" than you. When you are ever-present in and as all things you cannot have a void or a lack anywhere. You are Allness and as such there can be nothing else but you.

There is nothing other than you. You are all there is. Realising this deeply will bring profound love for all of creation because it is known to be you. The essence of everything is you. You are also all the shapes and forms too.

CHAPTER 7

Understanding Your
Wholeness Before Division

As usual, let's first check in and notice and be our formless Self. Looking and finding no objective self yet again, we can confirm that we are formless in our essential nature.

Take a look at this formlessness and see that it is what is hearing and perceiving the thoughts in your head. If you ask yourself "what hears this thought?" then you will be taken right back to this same formless you. That which hears thoughts is not affected by thoughts. How can you know this? If you look and confirm that thoughts arise out of this formless you, but they cannot affect you here. You are the source of all thoughts.

After thoughts arise, some are paid attention to and we begin to call them "my thoughts". But how can they be yours if they are arising out of you? Just as steam will rise out of a cup of hot water, so too thoughts arise out of you. The water is not deliberately causing steam to rise and neither do you force anything to manifest. Just like the hot water, it is your nature to allow things to manifest. If you see that thoughts arise out of you, then you can no longer believe that thoughts can trouble you. The water is not affected by the steam, and really the water and the steam are the same thing appearing in different ways. So too, you and the thoughts are the same thing.

Why is this important to grasp? Well if you can establish yourself as that formless presence that is before thought, you will no longer be able to divide yourself into a "me" and "everything else other than me". Division or separation can ONLY occur in thoughts. As soon as the thought "I forgot what I am" forms and is believed, we have a big journey on our hands which can seem to culminate in "I remember now what I am". But you are before thought. You are the place that cannot be touched by thoughts. Where would thoughts stick to anyway in the formless you?

Come to know experientially that you cannot be divided and that what you are is ALLNESS of the unmanifest, manifest and beyond that division and classification.

You are the All and the only thing that exists. Only later when thought comes and a body appears can there be separation and union with God, bondage and liberation.

CHAPTER 8

You Are the Unchanging One

Your true nature is not changing and you can begin to recognise that right now. Take a look at what is here right now. What are you? Not counting thoughts, feelings or anything else that comes and goes, look and see. There is something about you that simply is. It just is. It is not moving or growing, or becoming more. It simply is. Get to know this aspect of yourself, as it is you in your purest essence. Of course, you have a body, thoughts, feelings and a life – but this is your true home.

Spend some time just exploring what it is like to be this formless you. Notice that if you are formless, you are not changing. Only forms and shapes can change and move about. If we look at what we are in our purest essence, we will always come back to this formless essence.

The Root of All Fear

As human beings we live our lives against a backdrop of fear usually; a fear that is so deep within us and prevalent that we are not able to handle it consciously. This is the fear that one day we will begin to age, perhaps suffer from illness, disease and more challenges we can associate with older age, such as poverty and loneliness.

This fear comes from one very basic belief within us that we are separate entities, making our way through the world and that we were born and will one day die. The root of all fear is based upon this fear of annihilation or non-existence. It is not even feared so much that the body will die because we know that is true. The main root of this fear is that we think that without the body we will not be able to experience anymore.

As you read this, look again within yourself. Confirm yet again that you are not anywhere in particular, that you cannot find a separate entity called "me". Of course you exist, but not as a separate someone inside a body. Notice also that this sense of you is not changing. It is simply effortlessly here, noticing the thoughts, feelings and sensations coming in through the senses.

You are the Unchanging One

Contemplate over and over what it means that you are not changing. What does this mean for you? Can you age? Can you deteriorate over time? Will you suffer from the effects of an ageing body? Can you change?

You must drink deeply this knowledge again and again that you are not changing, because only then will it begin to have an effect upon you. You will begin to notice you are watching everything that happens to your body and are not affected by it. You are simply here, watching, not getting involved. Thoughts get involved but not you. Thoughts have opinions on what happens to the body but you witness those also.

Can you contract a disease? Can you have another birthday? Will you ever draw a pension? If you look deeply enough you will see that all these things are happening to your body and not you. If you are indeed the Unchanging One then it must be also true that you will stay just as you are right now. Eternally.

You will be just as you are right now – forever.

I do not mean you will feel the way you do right now, or that you will have the same thoughts forever. I mean you. As you really are. The Formless and Timeless One. This is what you will always be and even when this body fails you, then you will not be affected.

You are outside of time.

Or we could say that time is happening inside you.

Whichever statement feels most true to you now take it and contemplate it. If time is happening inside you then birth, life and death are also happening inside you and not TO you. You are the formless construct in which life happens. Bodies are being born inside you every moment. They are born, grow up, age and eventually die in you.

Death, illness, disease and ageing are concepts that simply do not apply to you.

CHAPTER 9

Recognising You Are The Absolute Awareness

One of the most common areas that we can feel stuck in realising we are the Awareness that never sleeps is this feeling that sometimes we are unaware. We might be trying to be the witness of a particular thought pattern or emotion that keeps coming up and most times we can simply observe. At some point our attention may drift and we may feel like we are the ones identifying with thoughts and acting them out. We will also feel strong emotions that correspond to the thoughts believed. This leads most people to complain that they simply "cannot be the awareness all the time".

A simple contemplation point can eradicate this belief that being aware is something we have to consciously do all the time. Nobody can keep aware as a separate person all the time, not even the Buddha.

Checking in to see again what we are will reveal once again that we are not a thing. We are no-thing. Things come and go, but not you. Things appear and disappear, but not you. Notice that you are constantly here.

When you begin to notice that you are always here when you look for you, you will recognise that you are always here and it is the waking state that is coming and going.

The waking state is superimposed upon you; it comes and goes but you do not. There is something that is aware even that the waking state has gone and it can report a lack of experiencing during sleep.

Checking in and seeing yourself to be formless and everywhere will begin to show you that you cannot be limited by time. What does this mean? It means that you must either be aware, or not. You cannot be aware one moment and then unaware the next moment.

Consciousness and unconsciousness are rotating states happening in front of you.

Contemplating the question "Can I ever be unaware?" will really take you into a deeper seeing of what you are. As you contemplate this question, stay with it until you reach a definite answer that does not need any external validation from a teacher. Consciousness is the waking state and unconsciousness is the sleep state and both are simply alternating for you, you watch them from your true place.

You will begin to see that you are beyond and before sleep *and* waking. When you look for yourself you always find something that is looking, that is aware. It is not in any particular location and yet it is looking.

28

Where are you looking from? You are the Seer of all this but where are you seeing from? Contemplate these questions and watch what is revealed to you.

You must want to see what you really are more than you want to still indulge in the idea that you are a person here on a spiritual search.

CHAPTER 10

Recognising You Are Sentience Itself

When we believe we are a separate person, a mind and body moving through our lives, we usually feel that we are either intelligent or not. We feel that the sum total of our sentience is between our ears as a capacity of our brain. We can feel that we are quite intelligent or we can feel that we have very little intellectual capability or anything in between.

Once we begin to discover our own formless nature as the True Self we must begin to redefine what sentience is. If we look in the dictionary, it will define sentience as "the capacity to feel, perceive or experience subjectively." But what is that capacity and where does it originate from?

Check in now and look for yourself as you read. Stop and tune in to the ever-present Reality that you are and notice it is you. You are aware, you know everything that is going on. At first it may be difficult to see why this is important for you to contemplate but as you investigate what you really are, you may make some huge discoveries.

This formless Self that you are is the source of all manifest beings and as such each human being has a sentience innate within them. For example, they know they exist, their name, sex, age etc. and can study many subjects intellectually and retain that knowledge in the mind.

You are not a sentient person. You are the source of sentience itself.

It is worthwhile spending some time contemplating this statement until you can confirm it is true experientially. This means you must keep looking at this until you know and see clearly that you are the awareness itself that is looking at the intellect, mind or thought. The knower of thought is not a thought. But what is it? What are you?

Once you have deeply contemplated this chapter, you will come to see that there is nothing else to find out or to know, because all knowing occurs only in the mind.

Intelligence, ignorance, knowing or not knowing come from the mind and that is happening in front of you.

If you contemplate what this means then you will begin to see that you are before and beyond ignorance and also knowledge. Ignorance in this context to not know what you are, or to be sure that you are a separate person (both are the same). Knowledge here means to know you are the formless Self. Both these states of ignorance and knowledge come from the mind and are happening in thought. If you realise this then it has a profound impact on you.

What does this mean? It means that all revelations, all insights, all "aha" moments, all breakthroughs are happening in the mind only and you remain always as you are − the perfection itself.

It may take a while before it fully impacts upon you how final this realisation is. It means that no matter how much meditation, contemplation and self-inquiry you do for the rest of this bodily existence, you will never improve upon, change or become more yourself.

You already are this perfect formless Awareness Self.

The paradox is that we do seem to need to use the mind to contemplate enough that we can finally come to see we are beyond, before and inside the mind. We are the source of knowing and understanding and as such are already complete, total and whole. We have never been on this journey of transcendence, letting go and in fact – we are not even the one who is waking up.

Once this revelation really begins to happen experientially, we can begin to live from the completion of the Self. We will see desires and suffering drop away in the seeing of our own "already-so-ness".

CHAPTER II

Seeing Your Wholeness Before Desire Arises

As human beings, we almost always want something from our lives. We usually want something to come to us that we have not as yet got or we want to get rid of something we have now. We can also want something to continue or stay in our lives that is destined to end or leave us. Most of our human suffering occurs because we spend a lot of our time fighting against what's happening to us, what happened before in the past or fearing wheat might happen in the future.

As we embark upon a spiritual path, most of us substitute all our normal desires for the urge and wish to wake up fully to the realisation of what we are. We may begin to suffer even more than we did before we heard about the True Self and enlightenment, and especially so if we have a glimpse or an experience of the awakened state. It is not uncommon for people to spend years desiring some particular state or meditating to try and become some idealised version of themselves that they would like to be.

The Truth is already present, whole and perfect. It has no desire and it cannot suffer. Only once we believe our thoughts again and feel we are a separate person can we once again suffer.

Stop for a moment and notice yourself just here, notice that you are simply here. As you are right now, you can perceive the body, thoughts perhaps, emotions maybe, and outer stimuli. But what you really are is here and not trying to get anywhere else.

Notice also that your real Self is simply being here. There is no separate person in this that you are to want anything or reject anything. Look again and again and be sure to confirm this until you see that all desires come from a rejection of the already perfect Self by the mind.

There are no desires possible when you are simply being yourself. Check in again and see that just as you are now, just here, you do not actually want anything or need anything.

Look again and confirm that you are effortlessly here and at peace just as you are right now. Nothing that you could acquire, receive or become can make this right here and now any better than it is. No experience or state that you could feel would impact and improve upon the real you that is simply present, aware and yet not affected by anything.

Even once this body that you are using to perceive yourself begins to fail you and eventually drops, you will be just as you always were.

Desire means you want or need something to be other than it is right now.

Having a desire is not wrong but we must also come to see that whatever we desire is really only so because we feel it will make us happier, more at peace or safer than we are right now. As we begin to investigate what we really are, we can come to the startling conclusion that nothing at all can alter, change or affect us. No thoughts, states, emotions or outer circumstances make even a slight change to the Already Perfect nature of the Self. You are invisible, formless and ever present; you are Reality itself and you need nothing at all to be happy. Even as you begin to contemplate the place where desire cannot reach you will see greater joy and contentment coming to you.

Confirm and re-confirm through looking, seeing and realising that you are not in need of anything, nor can you want anything. You do not even need to know who you are, as that would only be a thought happening in this that you are already. You are already all that you could desire to be. Everything that happens and manifests is included in this wholeness that is so total that it can even allow a sense of incompletion, inadequacy or unworthiness to be present.

You need nothing, all is arising in you. All is you.

CHAPTER 12

There Is Only Abundance

Most of us spend our lives chasing something that we want from the world, from ourselves and others. We always seem to be deficient in something that we need somehow; such as love, money, respect, time and many more things that seem to allude us. We have come to believe that abundance has an opposite and that lack or "not-enough-ness" is actually real. We never stop to question how much energy we expend trying to acquire more of whatever we seem to need and how that could be the very thing that is perpetuating the sense of lack and seeming absence of it.

Most of us have spent many years reaching for something that we do not feel we have as yet. This could be a worldly goal such as marriage, a family or job success. We can also spend as much time on an inner search for love, respect, acceptance or forgiveness. Even as spiritual seekers, we can spend much time and energy looking for awakening or enlightenment; trying hard to get to some state or place that we feel is not already here.

All of this can stop in a moment if we really begin to look and see what we actually are; we are not the body and mind that wants these things. We are the infinite formless Self that all things manifest in. We must begin to undo the idea that there is an opposite of abundance and that there can be anything other than plenitude. As we check in right now again, actually looking and seeing that what we are is formless and everywhere, we can see that we are unmanifest in our purest form and yet all things manifest inside the formless awareness that we are.

This formlessness has no boundaries or edges and goes on forever in all directions all around our bodies, inside and outside and even permeating the empty space in the room you are in. What we are is so all-pervading that we have not noticed it because it is everywhere at all times. The silent, invisible and intangible source of everything.

Notice right now that you are not located in a particular place. Notice also that something always has to manifest out of this unmanifest invisible Self that we are. No void is possible, even space is the first manifestation of this Self. Oxygen, air, space, planets, people, houses, cars, trees and so much more populates this awareness. If you continued to look throughout the known universe you would never find one single empty voidness where nothing has manifested.

What does this mean for us? It means that the Self knows only abundance, that it has no opposite, that there is no such thing as "off-ness", lack or limitation. It means the unmanifest must ALWAYS show up as something. It has no other option. It must manifest as a range of things from the more intangible space in the room to the more tangible thoughts and emotions and finally to heavy and dense objects like our bodies, planets, and more.

Something has to appear in this "not-yet-something-ness" that we are. So what determines what shows up? We do! What we believe is possible or impossible determines what will manifest. What has already manifested perpetuates our thoughts about it and therefore whether we are likely to get more of the same over and over. Once we see this, however, we are not limited by it anymore.

We have all been manifesting an abundance of seeming lack!

If you contemplate your life you will see that the more you notice a lack of something, the more lack you get. It is obvious with money or time or patience, for example.

Once we see that abundance is the only option in the Allness that is everywhere and that something MUST show up in this Emptiness that we are, then we can begin to allow the highest possibility to manifest. We are always seeing the highest possibility manifested from the unmanifest. We are always shaping what will become form out of the formless. Everywhere, at all times, something is in a state of becoming.

We can begin to recognise that the only option in Reality is for the unmanifest to manifest on full power. It is always expressing itself at 100% of its capability to do so. Everything that has appeared in this vast awareness is whole and total and already perfect. Each thing is a perfect example of itself, and if we can begin to see this, we can experience more peace, love and joy. How do we do that? Simply by knowing that what we think is lacking is actually waiting to be selected as an option, rather than missing.

The unmanifest, formless awareness that we are is really like an infinite ocean of possibilities, but not having become an actuality as yet. When we simply are our formless Self, then quite naturally the most expansive, joyous and abundant possibility will move into actuality or become manifest. The universe is always the highest manifestation that is possible in that moment. Whenever we begin to shape and mould what will manifest with our expectations, whether positive or negative, we begin to limit the number of available possibilities from an infinite number to just a small few. Therefore, what we think about our reality shapes what we actually experience, but it cannot change what we actually are.

(Note: If you are scientifically minded this also fits with Heisenberg's Uncertainty Principle. The only difference is that the level of consciousness of the observer is what collapses the wave function into actuality based on its inherent power. The higher the level of consciousness of the observer, the greater the possibility available in the sea of infinite possibility and higher choices become probabilities rather than just possibilities.)

Simply said, we are going to get an abundance of something, even if it is an abundance of lack! Stay as your true Self before the manifestation, as the unmanifest Self, and watch the most beautiful manifestation occur spontaneously. It will begin to surprise and delight you. You must begin to choose what you wish to see happen by knowing that possibility is waiting to show up for you and you need do nothing for that to happen. We must disregard any appearance of lack in our lives as simply the abundance we desire having already shown up in a different way. Appearance of lack is not the same as actual lack! Lack, void or absence is the one thing that Self cannot do! Contemplate this deeply.

CHAPTER 13

Recognising You Are the Undivided One Which Includes All Things

Once again, take a minute to look at yourself as you really are. Notice when you search for yourself you find only a sense of you being here that you cannot touch, taste or feel and yet you are very much present. Notice also that you cannot find anything other than you; meaning you find only one thing which is you. Although this may sound obvious, it is worth looking at deeper.

What does it mean that you are the only one you can find? First, take a moment to check and see if you can find an end to you. You will not be able to find the end of you and yet you will seem to be only experiencing through this body and mind. We will have a knowing that we must be everywhere if we look closer at this. If we do not end and have no boundaries where you end and I begin, then how can there be anything other than you? I must be you, anyone who reads this book must be also you and everything you see must also be you.

As you let the implications of this seeing come to the surface you may find yourself feeling a little overwhelmed at first. Allow these feelings to come and know that you are revealing yourSelf to yourself, and as such it can feel strange at first. For so long we have thought of ourselves as being only here in this body. When this belief begins to loosen its hold over us, it can feel like our whole life experience is changing.

It is important to notice that the Wholeness that you are is the formless you that you have been noticing, but also all the forms that appear in you too. We cannot discount the manifestations as being unreal or not important because they are arising out of you. We can begin to see that every thought, feeling, opinion, and experience is also us and must be included in our definition of what we are. We must be mature enough to see that all that arises inside us IS us. I do not mean only the feelings and thoughts that happen inside your body, but inside all bodies – and in fact inside the You that is everywhere. What does that exclude then as "not you"? Nothing at all. It is all you, every last bit of it is you.

All of creation is you, showing up as various appearances inside you. All that ever was, is and will be is you showing up in various different forms. All that will ever be born, live and die for the rest of eternity is you also.

Take a moment to contemplate that and although it may be difficult to accept, it can be experientially realised if you are willing to stay with this most important subject.

What are the implications in everyday life of this amazing revelation? It means that everything is you and you can no longer blame, judge or keep yourself separate from it. You must begin to take all that is inside you and realise it is all you. I am not speaking here about blaming yourself for some atrocity that happens across the other side of the world; I am simply asking you to come to see that you can show up in many forms. Some enlightened and compassionate and some hateful, deluded and unloving, and all possibilities in-between. This is not a personal thing; it is seeing yourself impersonally.

What can you include in yourself now from this seeing rather than pushing away?

- We can come to include all the people we do not like as being us too.
- All those we hate and hate us.
- All the resistance that appears inside us.
- All the positive and good things we have done.
- All the good things others have done to help us is also us.
- We must also begin to include God inside us, AS us.
- We must realise also that all the Awakened Beings, Sages and Teachers we love are also simply appearances inside us.
- All the things we wish to get rid of, such as attachments and all else is simply us showing up in a manifest form.

When this seeing begins to flower and open for you then you will feel less and less fear; for what is there to be scared of if it is all you? What can hurt you or attack you if it is all you?

CHAPTER 14

Seeing Your Infinite Nature

The more we can slow down and take a moment on a regular basis to look and confirm we are formless, the easier this process of coming to live as we really are will be. It may be challenging to accept at first that we are formless, everywhere and all-pervading because we have been taught to value thought and experience more than anything else.

In this chapter we are going to look at how we come to see we are infinite. Infinite means that you go on forever, without limitation or ending and without boundaries. How can we come to know we are ALL? How can we come to live as the Allness that includes the unmanifest and the manifest? To understand this on a level deeper than the mind only, we must begin to look in a different way. We cannot use the mind to understand what we are, because it simply cannot. Even if we have the thought realisation that "I am the Allness/Self" then we are still *thinking* about the Self and not actually *being* it.

The key is to understand the limitations of our mind and why it cannot go beyond time and space. Our mind is really a mechanism for sorting, classifying and analysing. It is a labelling machine; it might see objects through our physical eyes and it might say "bike", "fish" or anything that we can perceive. It might smell something through the nose and say "smoke". Our mind takes feedback from the senses and labels it. We can begin to see that our mind can only think ABOUT something but not actually experience it. A name or a label is really an abstraction of the thing itself; it is a concept to describe and define but does not actually mean anything unless it is compared to something else.

When we experience something from the viewpoint of thought it gives the illusion that we are someone, here, in this body that is located in a particular place in time and space. The more we have these experiences, the greater our sense of being separate, of being someone is. But if we check in again to our real Self that just simply is here, we will not find an object. We will find a subjective sense of awareness. Something is watching and observing – that something is you.

We can miss seeing who we really are time after time, if we expect to see an object; to have an "aha" moment or realisation about something. We must instead learn to perceive what cannot be sensed, seen, felt, heard or touched and yet that is what we really are. A person looking from a particular point in time and space cannot ever perceive the Wholeness. An object cannot perceive the subject. The witnessed cannot perceive the witness.

As this begins to sink it deeper into our consciousness we can come to see that we are the formless awareness looking through each body. We must come to a greater realisation that we are looking, experiencing through all the bodies all at once. Each individual body cannot experience the

Wholeness, but the Wholeness can experience itself through each and every body. The formless awareness is aware of whatever experience is happening in every manifest form. Some forms, such as humans, are much more aware of their surroundings and in human beings, the formlessness can come to a true seeing of what it actually is. This is happening right now as you read this!

In other forms such as planets, rocks, air, tables and chairs it is not self-aware at all, but it is still experiencing "table-ness" and what it is like to be a tree or a bird. In this way you can come to see that you are experiencing all of it, all the time, bodies come and go, but you are watching from everywhere and watching all the time.

Mind will resist this and want to stop at a thought realisation but you must come to value the seeing as the Noumenon, as the Allness, as the Self rather than as a separate person.

Let's keep this simple and once again check in and confirm that we cannot find ourselves in any particular place. As you scan for your being and its location, the most we can really say is that we are here, but "here" in this sense now means subjectively watching and not here in a particular body only.

We can say that we are here and everywhere; meaning we are the Allness itself perceiving through all of creation and we also SEEM to be here in this body too, experiencing as a person moving about in time and space, progressing on a journey and becoming more aware of ourselves. Which one is more real? Well at first the viewpoint of looking from everywhere will seem unreal, strange and hard to grasp hold of and understand. The idea that you are someone trying to understand the great Self will seem obvious and you might meet resistance when you try to question it. Over time and with consistent interest and curiosity this will turn right around so that you can always know you are everywhere and the sense you are a someone here in this body perceiving will seem as though it is now light, superficial and is there for a kind of functionality so that you can interact with "others". You know there are no others but you also know that there might always seem to be! Can you handle this paradox? Yes you can, it is only how you have always been!

Mind eventually comes to a stop all by itself when we begin to see that the Real Self that we are is not thinking at all, it is the pure and undisturbed Witness of all. You cannot be the Allness experientially and still have a busy mind. If your mind is still busy it simply means you are not yet fully living as the Self and more contemplation must be done.

CHAPTER 15

Conclusion

Contemplating one of these chapters over and over, or all of them, is enough to cause a profound and powerful shift in your sense of self. It will begin to change how you perceive yourself from someone to being Pure Awareness. It is easy to come to a thought-based understanding of what we are and to know all about the Allness; but few are the ones that make it all the way to living as the Sages do. This is the purpose of this book and it will help you to structure your contemplation and deepen your seeing.

This book is meant to build upon itself so as you work on the contemplations in chapter 5, for example, you are simultaneously working on all the chapters. Each chapter will give you greater and greater clarity and you will fall in love with what you really are.

You would not be reading this book if you were not destined to wake up fully, beyond all thought and mind, to be a light in this world to others seeking what you have become. You would not be reading this now if your Enlightenment was not already in the cards. Take the time to look, see, confirm what you are and question every assumption, doubt and block your mind seems to put up in front of you.

Find a teacher to help guide you too and stay open to help along the way. These words can help awaken a truth within your heart but you must do the work to fully realise it; otherwise these are just words on a page of a book you read once and put away. People often ask me for the "how to" of full awakening but few take this advice and follow it fully until all suffering has stopped. Are you one of them?

APPENDIX

Summary of Common Names For the Noumenon

Below are some of the ways the Noumenon has been described in other teachings. For each set of terms there are two names. Reading through the list may help to awaken a recognition in you as you read and at certain times along the way different sets of terms may be more appealing than others.

They are all names for That Which Has No Name. Don't get attached to any name; look at what the name points to.

NOUMENON	PHENOMENA
Oneness	many
Allness	separation
Empty Mind	full mind
Unity	multiplicity
Silent Mind	noisy mind
Non-Duality	duality

"I" as Consciousness	"I" as a person
Nothingness	somethingness
Awakeness	sleep/dream
Consciousness	unconsciousness
Silence	sound
Subjectivity	object
Being	being someone/something
Stillness	movement
Presence	person
God	ego
Truth	falsehood
Formless	form
Reality	illusion
Knowingness	knowing about
Awareness	perception
Context	content
Infinite Field	finite being
Timeless	duration

If you would like more information about Helen, her live Satsangs, silent retreats and classes please contact us:

Visit our website at **www.helenhamilton.org**

Find us on facebook by searching @satsangwithhelenhamilton

Search for us on YouTube: satsangwithhelenhamilton

Email us at evolutionofspirit@gmail.com

Printed in Great Britain
by Amazon

59885780R00040

6

INSTANT PRESENCE: ALLOWING NATURAL MEDITATION TO HAPPEN

"To realize the inexpressible truth, do not manipulate mind or body but simply open into transparency with relaxed, natural grace."

— *Tilopa*

In our day-to-day life, we are almost always habitually involved with thoughts and projections, constantly trying to manipulate whatever comes up in our life experiences by either moving toward the ones we like or moving away from the ones we don't.

The thoughts themselves are not the problem. The problem is that we are constantly reacting to them and so every thought that arises in the mind continually distracts us, "seemingly" obscuring our true nature - natural awareness. By natural awareness here I refer to our true naked nature, stripped bare of these movements of the mind. Since the mind depends on this constant movement for its continued existence, the practice of *Instant Presence* is to be internally still and undistracted. This actually means to leave everything that arises in our experience (thoughts, sights, sounds and sensations) as it is, without manipulations or strategies. We simply relax in the present moment without trying to improve it, correct it or replace it.

This is not a passive surrender but a letting go to being totally present and totally relaxed at the same time, without any artificiality or manipulation. Instead of our usual habit of grasping and making the moment solid, we open, dissolve and "let everything be".

Essentially, this is the complete practice. There is nothing else that we are doing.

STOP ALL MOVEMENT AND LET SPONTANEOUS PRESENCE BE

The practice of *Instant Presence* is an opening, a relaxing of our focus (while maintaining alertness) and letting everything come to us instead of us chasing after something (even though the reality is that awareness doesn't "come" to us because we already are that).

The words "relaxing into it while maintaining alertness" seem to point to a mind-made effort, but what I'm talking about is to leave the mind as it is, without giving it anything to do.

We don't strive to reach some "amazing goal" or some "advanced state." Nor do we use the practice to "go deep into ourselves" or to withdraw from the world. All of that only obstructs the free flow of our natural state and conditions us to believe that our already enlightened nature is somewhere other than right where we are, as we are, right now.

Instead, we just trust, connect, and realize what is already here.

LUMINOUS COGNIZING EMPTINESS

The practice of *Instant Presence* is simply to remain undistracted from present wakefulness, to relax and open in all directions, without spacing out and losing our alertness.

To be as open and relaxed as possible while being present and lucid with all our senses wide open. This is the marriage between emptiness, spaciousness (the female aspect of awareness) and the knowingness or cognizing aspect (the male part).

Straying too far into the empty aspect of our true nature makes us spaced out, ungrounded and foggy. Relaxed awareness is neither spacey nor hazy. It needs to be alert and vivid, not like a drug-induced state or a dream. If we move too far in that direction we start losing interest in everything. On the other hand, when we stray too far into the knowingness aspect, we become uptight and controlling of our experience, we forget the emptiness aspect of our nature and we become caught up in the world.

How can we find the right balance between the two? First, if possible, give up all effort and rest in the total effortlessness of this awareness now. If distractions happen, use the minimum of "effort" necessary to be clear and awake while letting things be, without trying to change or modify them.

Once the light of awareness is switched on, remember to let go of the switch and return to formless awareness or you will just keep switching the light on and off. Just let go of the switch and the one switching it on and off.

Rest in what is, this moment – just accept it and be in harmony with the moment as it is.

WHAT THE PRACTICE OF INSTANT PRESENCE IS IN A NUTSHELL

In this practice we simply rest in a natural, effortless way without manipulations or strategies.

We take a break from making anything happen or not happen. We are not trying to be anything or anyone, nor attempting to change or accomplish anything. We are just resting in what is happening moment by moment.

We rest directly in the spontaneity of our natural, unadulterated being, without fabricating, rejecting or changing anything.

Effortlessly, without thinking or trying to figure anything out, we allow everything that arises in our experience (thoughts, sights, sounds and sensations) to be as it is.

We don't choose the thoughts, feelings, or experiences that come into awareness but rather meet them when they do, without judgment.

We rest in silence, as the silence. This silence is beginningless and endless and our body and the world are here in this spacious awareness, permeated with the sound of vibrant silence.

We simply rest as awareness, aware of itself.

~ ~ ~

Since awareness is not an object, I realize it is impossible for me to focus on it. Therefore, what might help me is to steer my attention away from sensations and thoughts. Am I correct in moving in this direction?

Indeed you are. You are definitely on the right track; however, you cannot use your will to steer your attention away from your thoughts. The reason is because this in itself is a thought. Instead, just notice what is going on.

When you attempt to focus by "un-focusing," you are operating at the level of the mind. Doing this will not really help you recognize awareness. This "practice" of resting in awareness is not a training to get rid of thought; it is being free of involvement with thoughts.

Awareness is the formless, timeless, and eternal space within which all the thoughts you have about it and all of the practices you perform in an attempt to attain it, have their existence.

~ ~ ~

Where do I keep my focus during the practice of *Instant Presence* ?

We do not focus inwardly, outwardly or anywhere in-between. We stop all movement towards anything and let spontaneous presence just be. This frees us from the witness and the witnessed, the doer and the deed and what is left is the true nature of both.

~ ~ ~

Must we surrender our ego to truly experience the truth of our real nature? And if so, what does that involve?

Ego just means the personalization of everything, the identification with a separate entity. Once the recognition that who we are as this all-pervading awareness has occurred, the notion that the ego is separate from awareness begins to dissolve. Then the ego is seen not as an enemy, but simply as an aspect of the source. It is realized that there is only That, the Absolute, the One without a second, unfolding in the shape and form of the ordinary.

The classic example is the ocean and its many expressions as wave, foam or spray. Regardless of the form the water takes, it is still ocean.

The source that is functioning through the saint and the sinner, the drug addict and the monk, the psychopath and the guru, is the same. Sometimes the expression of that source is ugly, sometimes beautiful, sometimes tragic, and sometimes blissful.

It's only the ego that wants to surrender the ego; the real meaning of surrender does not involve anything external. It means to surrender to your true nature.

To surrender is to relax and accept without resistance that your true nature is the totality of being. Surrender is a letting go, a releasing of the ego's hold on what it thinks is reality.

It is letting go of all notions and opinions of what the world is and how it works, and the belief that what our mind creates is real. It is the allowing of the person we thought we were to die.

How? By forgetting everything we ever thought we knew about the ego and who we think or believe we are.

Do this, and the ego goes with it.